P9-CQV-028

THE 16-BAR
THEATRE AUDITION

100 SONGS EXCERPTED FOR SUCCESSFUL AUDITIONS

COMPILED AND EDITED BY MICHAEL DANSICKER

ISBN 0-634-06441-X

HAL•LEONARD®
CORPORATION
7777 W. BLUEMOUND RD. P.O. BOX 13819 MILWAUKEE, WI 53213

Visit Hal Leonard Online at
www.halleonard.com

CONTENTS

*Songs not from shows

SHOW INDEX

PREFACE

After completing coursework in musical theatre degree programs at universities and conservatories, a very large number of musical theatre graduates, along with other young hopefuls, head for New York City. Their ultimate goal, of course, is a career in the professional musical theatre. Most young actors do not get immediate representation from agents or managers, who can secure for their clients a private appointment with a show's creative team. The standard "open singer's call" has become the most readily available opportunity for thousands of aspiring performers. It provides actors a chance to be heard and considered for work in various venues, from theme park/cruise line shows to Equity Broadway productions.

While directors, choreographers and casting offices are always anxious to discover new talent, audition time continues to be severely limited. Massive turnouts have become "the norm." In order to accommodate the crowds, the audition monitor will frequently announce the casting director's request for a 16-bar excerpt at a singing call. The concept of editing music for auditions becomes a frightening prospect to those not experienced in streamlining their selection on short notice. It is a task that takes musical experience and some careful thought!

WHY 16 BARS?

In the world of popular song writing, the standard 32-bar song form (AABA) has been the backbone of composition for decades. In this context, a 16-bar excerpt would imply half of a song. Prior to about 1970, Broadway shows were vehicles to supply the world with dance tunes and popular music. While the musical selections served the plot and characters of their shows, the songs were also written to have an extended life outside of the theatre. Today there is virtually no crossover from Broadway to the popular music market. Contemporary theatre composers and lyricists do not adhere to traditional structures, commercial form, or content in their work. Their writing faithfully serves the drama they are musicalizing, but it is not easily consolidated for an audition excerpt.

It is not always easy to decide on a 16-bar selection from a song. *The choice should not be arbitrary. You should always choose the best 16 bars!* This could be the verse, the bridge of the song, or an extended coda tagged on to your selected piece. You have to find out what works best for you. Your selection should time between 20 and 30 seconds. *No longer!* In most cases 16 bars is the right amount of music, although occasionally 32 bars will be more appropriate if the selection is in a very fast cut time, or "in 1." If you can communicate effectively to the audition panel in a shorter cutting, such as 8 or 12 bars, then do so! The piano introduction to your singing should be very limited, usually a one-note "bell tone" or one bar. It is not out of line to request your starting pitch when you speak with the pianist. Make sure you clearly communicate the tempo to the audition pianist. Your music should be clearly marked. Any transposition should be neatly written out. Do not expect the accompanist to transpose at sight. Material from showcases, camp shows and college revues should be left at home. Discordant arrangements and bizarre novelty tunes are of little use in 16-bar auditions. Of course, pass over songs that include extended orchestral solos.

BASIC PRESENTATION

You must impart your complete understanding of the music and lyrics you have selected. Your negotiation of the musical phrase and ability to be specific with acting elements are very important. Good singing technique is, of course, essential (placement, breath control and pitch). Your connection with the dramatic integrity of the piece is also important. The song should be presented honestly and thoughtfully. Be familiar with the shows you are auditioning for! Your music should reflect the style and spirit of the musical being cast. Dialects should be avoided; unless told otherwise, sing in English! It is never wise to interpolate unlikely notes to show off the upper limits of your vocal range. If a composer, or a firm performing tradition, has given an optional high note, feel free to use it. However, a disembodied "howl" with no cohesive relation to the phrase will surely not work favorably for you. While the rigor of a competitive audition experience can take its toll, always impart a sense of total commitment to your work, and the joy of being a musical theatre actor.

VOCAL RANGES

On Broadway today, the baritone has become a bari-tenor. A solid high F is imperative; a G is better. Basses should have an audible low F. Sopranos are sometimes asked for high D's, and belters now go as high as F. Tenors many times are asked for high C. But these are the extreme limits of range. At best, a 16-bar selection serves as an introduction to your vocal/acting skills. Do what is comfortable for you. If you are to be considered for a position in a production, further exploration of your vocal ability will take place in a callback situation. *You can't show everything in 16 bars!* Tenors should feel free to use selections from the baritone volume. Ladies should be ready to show the legit (soprano) and belt aspects of their voices if asked. Always have an alternate selection ready.

DANCERS

The dancer's call is a bit different than an open singer's call. The singing portion of the dancer audition is held only after the dancers have learned the presented movement combination and made their way through an elimination process. While many dancers in New York can hold their own at any singer call, the creative team will be a bit more flexible with dancers for the singing portion of the audition.

THE SELECTIONS IN THESE VOLUMES

The repertoire of the Broadway musical remains abundant and diversified, but large segments of material remain under-utilized. I have included selections from Broadway musicals, operettas, and pop hits. I gravitated to writers of outstanding talent and exceptional merit. A well-written song is a tremendous asset to any performer. No individual will be able to use all 100 excerpts in a particular anthology! There are songs that demand leading lady and leading man stature, as well as character and comic selections. There are pieces that have enormous vocal range, and many that are just rhythmic and charming. It is your job to peruse the contents and find what you consider the right songs for your needs. I have heard all of this material used to great advantage at many auditions. I have attempted to edit and indicate the most effective cuttings, trying to avoid phrase interruption. I have chosen what I feel are the most suitable keys, however, do not be afraid to experiment with the key (but have it written out to take to the audition!). Do not be afraid to use a song that is commonly heard at auditions. It is important that your "take" on the material be intelligent and professional. Every actor is unique, and those listening to your audition will not object to hearing a song again.

AUDITIONING

The only way to secure a job in legitimate musical theatre is through a live audition. Everyone auditions! Some actors audition better than others. The audition process is one that takes time to hone, polish and perfect. While many successful film and television actors secure continuous employment via a compilation reel of their media exposure, stage actors must book via a live audition. Be honest in evaluating the success of each audition, and study how it can be improved in the future. Also take note of the people you are auditioning for, and keep this information in a journal for future reference. Continue studying voice and working with a vocal coach. Dance and acting classes are essential for keeping your work sharp and at a high, professional level.

I hope these editions of 16-bar selections will be helpful to actors planning to audition for any musical show. *It is very important that you also learn the entire song after you master the 16-bar excerpt.* There is always a chance that someone on the creative team will say, "That was great; let's hear the whole song!" *Be prepared.*

Michael Dansicker
New York City
December, 2003

MICHAEL DANSICKER has worked as arranger, composer, musical director, and pianist on over 100 Broadway and Off-Broadway productions, from *Grease* (1975) to *Dance of the Vampires* (2003). He has composed original music for over a dozen plays in New York, including *The Glass Menagerie* (revival with Jessica Tandy) and *Total Abandon* (with Richard Dreyfus), and musically supervised the Royal Shakespeare Company transfers of *Piaf*, *Good*, and *Les Liaisons Dangereuses*. He served as vocal consultant to the hit films *Elf* (New Line Cinema), *Analyze That!* (Warner Bros.), and *Meet the Parents* (Universal), and also scored the dance sequences for Paramount's comedy classic *Brain Donors* (starring John Turturro). In the world of concert dance, he has composed and scored pieces for Twyla Tharp, American Ballet Theatre, Geoffrey Holder, Mikhail Baryshnikov, and The Joffrey, as well as serving as pianist to Jerome Robbins and Agnes DeMille. Michael currently works as creative consultant to Walt Disney Entertainment. He composed the music for "The Audition Suite" (lyrics by Martin Charnin), published by Hal Leonard Corporation. As a vocal coach, he works with the top talent in New York and Hollywood (including Sony's pop division). As an audition pianist, he works regularly with important casting directors on both coasts, and for 15 years has played all major auditions for Jay Binder, the "dean" of Broadway casting. Mr. Dansicker's original music is licensed by BMI. He holds a MA from the Catholic University of America.

Excerpt # ALL ABOARD FOR BROADWAY

from *George M!*

Words and Music by
GEORGE M. COHAN

For the complete song see: HL00008203 *George M!* vocal selections.

think of all the fun I'll miss if I miss _____ that

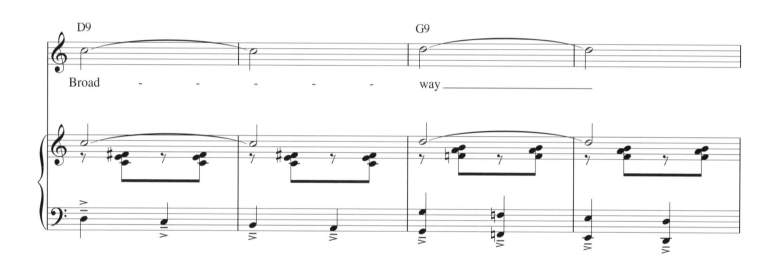

Broad - - - - - way _____

train. _____

ALWAYS TRUE TO YOU
IN MY FASHION

from *Kiss Me, Kate*

Words and Music by
COLE PORTER

Medium bounce

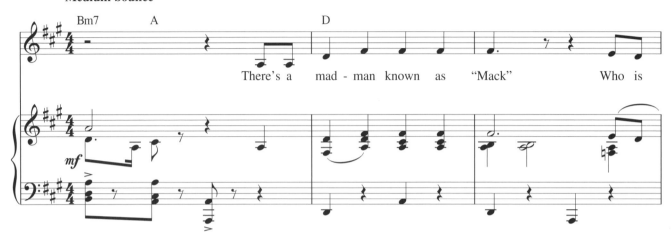

There's a mad-man known as "Mack" Who is

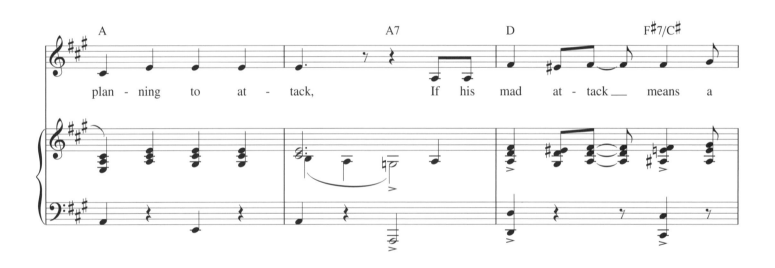

plan-ning to at-tack, If his mad at-tack___ means a

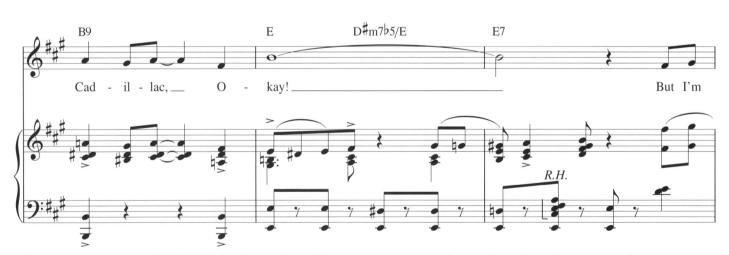

Cad-il-lac,___ O - kay!_____ But I'm

For the complete song see: HL00361072 *The Singer's Musical Theatre Anthology, Mezzo-Soprano/Belter Vol. 1 (Revised)*, and other sources.

AND ALL THAT JAZZ
from *Chicago*

Words by FRED EBB
Music by JOHN KANDER

Moderately slow, deliberately

For the complete song see: HL00303080 *And All That Jazz* piano/vocal/sheet music, and other sources.

ANOTHER OP'NIN', ANOTHER SHOW

Excerpt

from *Kiss Me, Kate*

Words and Music by
COLE PORTER

For the complete song see: HL00303110 *Another Op'nin', Another Show* piano/vocal sheet music, and other sources.

AS LONG AS HE NEEDS ME

from the Columbia Pictures - Romulus Motion Picture Production
of Lionel Bart's *Oliver!*

Words and Music by
LIONEL BART

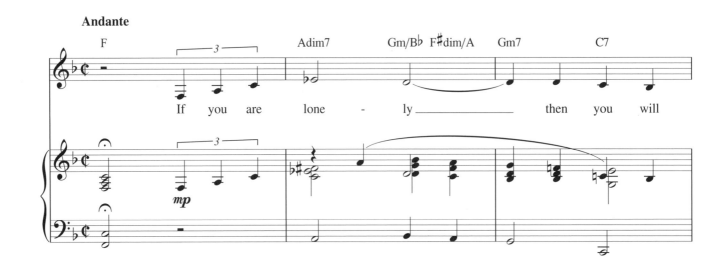

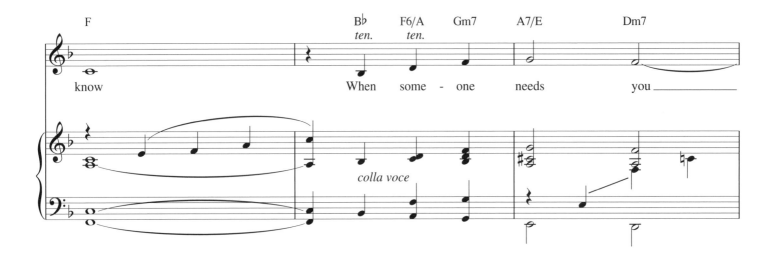

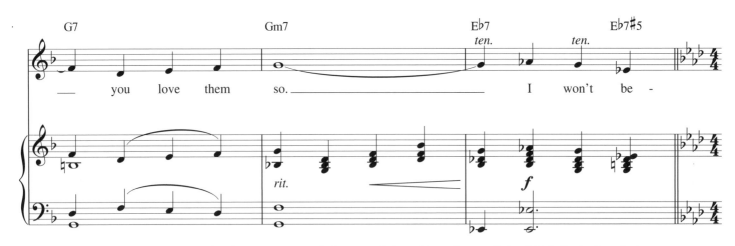

For the complete song see: HL00747031 *The Singer's Musical Theatre Anthology, Mezzo-Soprano/Belter Vol. 2 (Revised)*, and other sources.

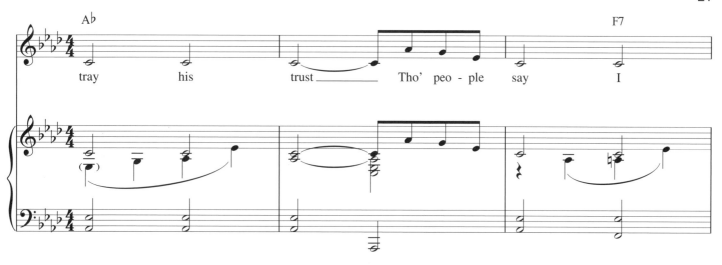

tray his trust _____ Tho' peo - ple say I

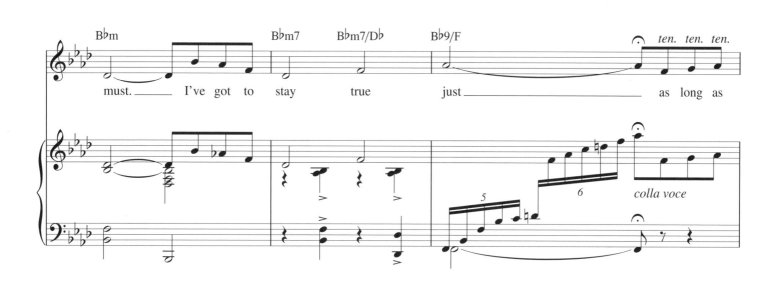

must. _____ I've got to stay true just _____ as long as

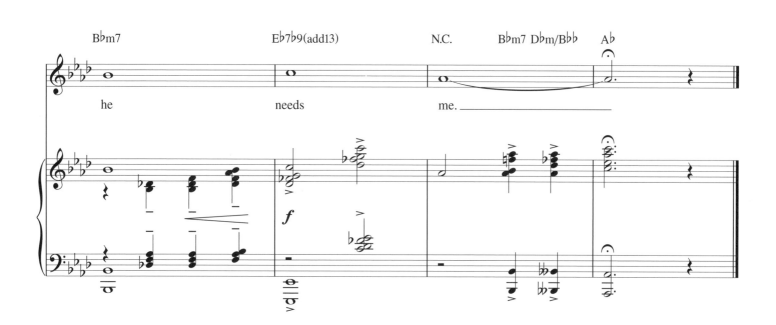

he needs me. _____

AT THE BALLET
from *A Chorus Line*

Music by MARVIN HAMLISCH
Lyrics by EDWARD KLEBAN

For the complete song see: HL00383312 *A Chorus Line* vocal selections, and other sources.

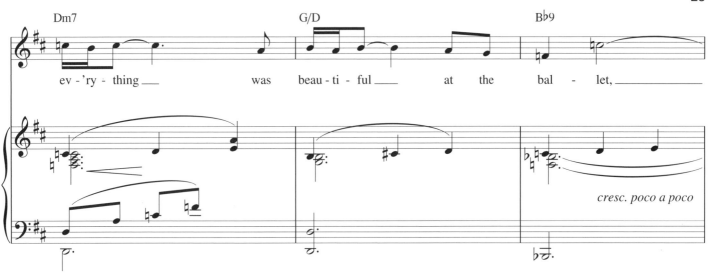

ev -'ry - thing ___ was beau -ti - ful ___ at the bal - let, ___

cresc. poco a poco

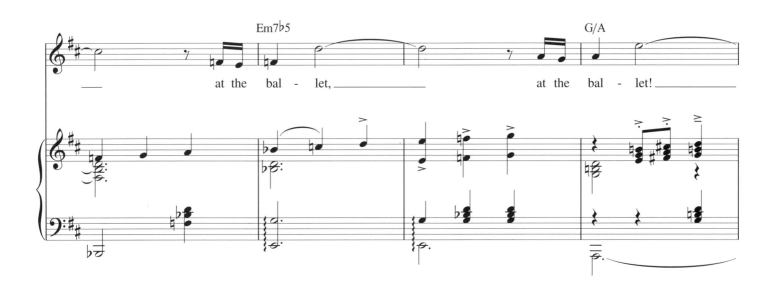

at the bal - let, _____ at the bal - let! ___

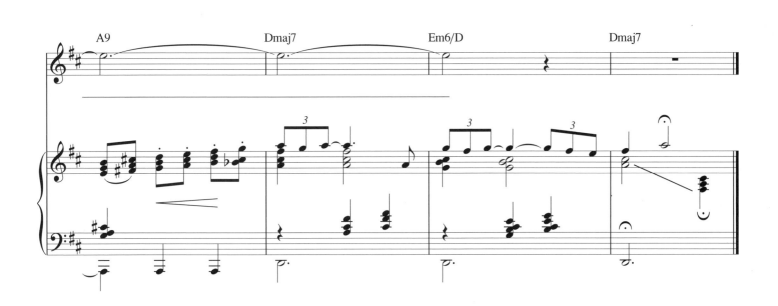

BEFORE THE PARADE PASSES BY

Excerpt

from *Hello, Dolly!*

Music and Lyric by
JERRY HERMAN

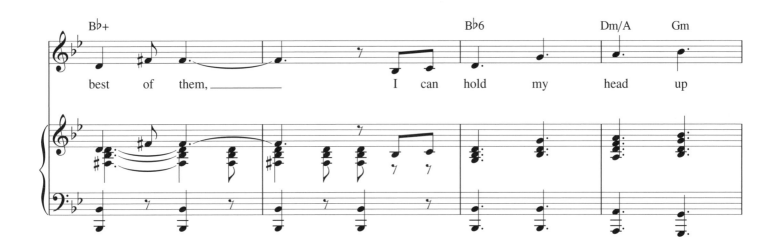

For the complete song see: HL00383730 *Hello, Dolly!* vocal selections, and other sources.

Excerpt

BETTER
from *A Class Act*

Words and Music by
EDWARD KLEBAN

For the complete song see: HL00313192 *A Class Act* vocal selections.

CAN YOU FEEL THE LOVE TONIGHT

Excerpt

Disney Presents *The Lion King: The Broadway Musical*

Music by ELTON JOHN
Lyrics by TIM RICE

For the complete song see: HL00353393 *Can You Feel the Love Tonight?* piano/vocal sheet music, and other sources.

BROADWAY BABY
from *Follies*

Words and Music by
STEPHEN SONDHEIM

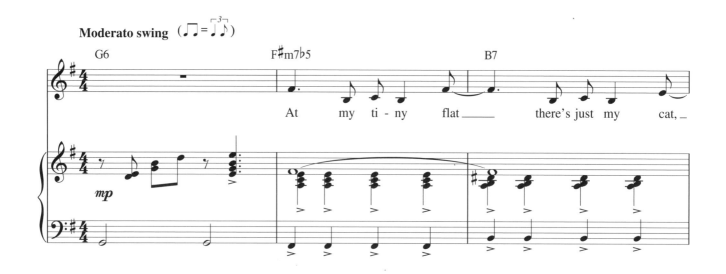

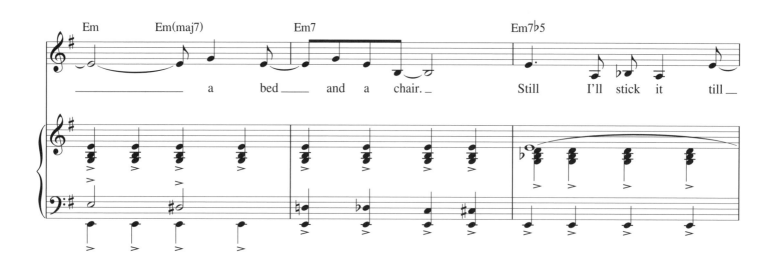

For the complete song see: HL00361072 *The Singer's Musical Theatre Anthology, Mezzo-Soprano/Belter Vol. 1 (Revised),* and other sources.

Excerpt

A CHANGE IN ME

from *Walt Disney's Beauty and the Beast: The Broadway Musical*

Words by TIM RICE
Music by ALAN MENKEN

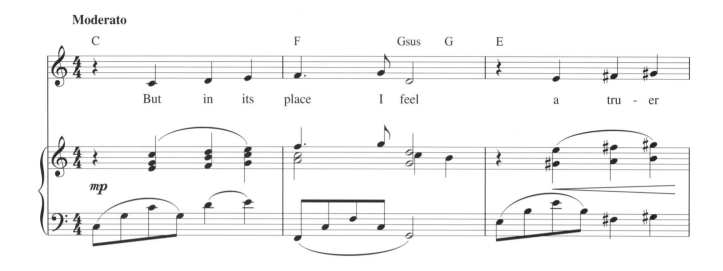

For the complete song see: HL00740123 *The Singer's Musical Theatre Anthology, Mezzo-Soprano/Belter Vol. 3,* and other sources.

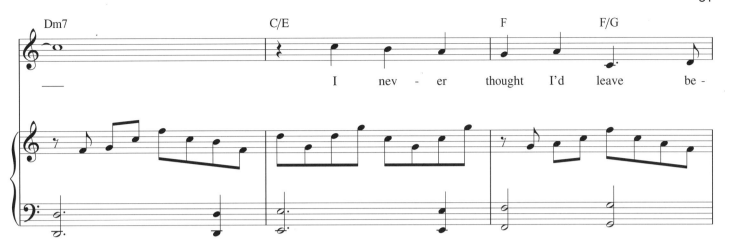

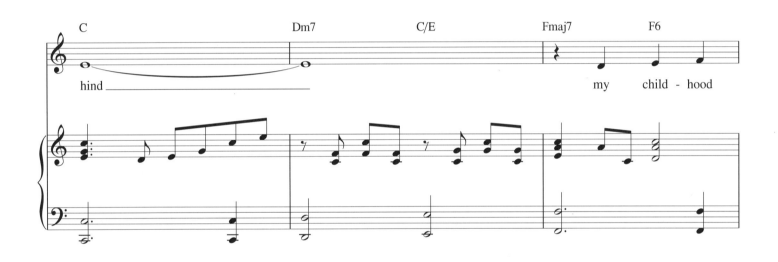

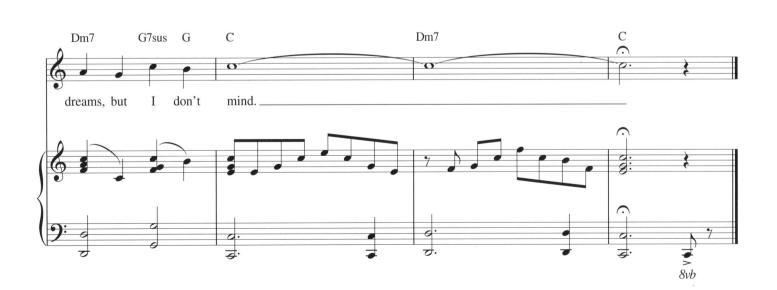

COLORS OF THE WIND
from *Walt Disney's Pocahontas*

Music by ALAN MENKEN
Lyrics by STEPHEN SCHWARTZ

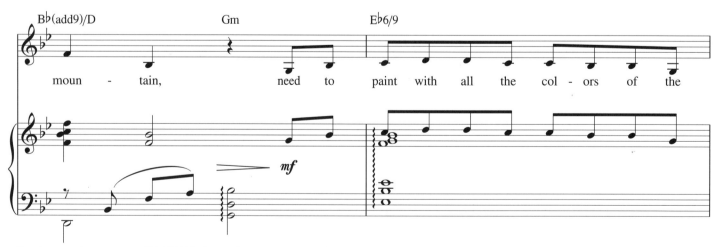

For the complete song see: HL00313013 *Pocahontas* vocal selections, and other sources.

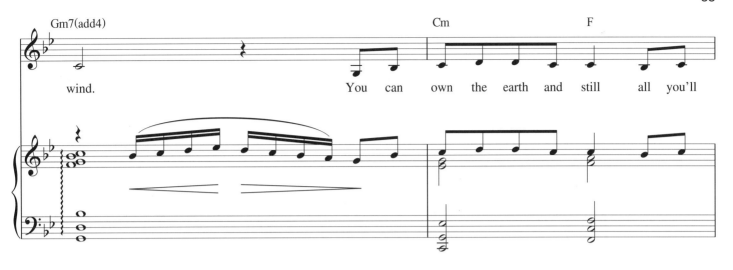

wind.　You can own the earth and still all you'll

own is earth un - til　you can paint with all the co - lors of the　wind._____

rit. e cresc.　　*f > mp*　　*a tempo*

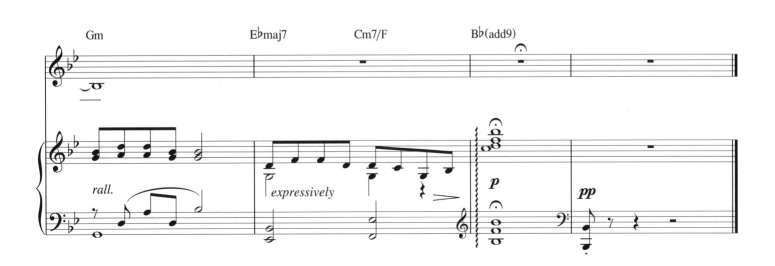

rall.　　*expressively*　　*p*　　*pp*

DISNEYLAND
from *Smile*

Words by HOWARD ASHMAN
Music by MARVIN HAMLISCH

For the complete song see: HL00740157 *Musical Theatre Anthology for Teens - Young Women's Edition.*

DON'T RAIN ON MY PARADE
from *Funny Girl*

Words by BOB MERRILL
Music by JULE STYNE

For the complete song see: HL00740123 *The Singer's Musical Theatre Anthology, Mezzo-Soprano/Belter Vol. 3,* and other sources.

DON'T TELL MAMA
from the Musical *Cabaret*

Words by FRED EBB
Music by JOHN KANDER

For the complete song see: HL00361072 *The Singer's Musical Theatre Anthology, Mezzo-Soprano/Belter Vol. 1 (Revised),* and other sources.

EVERYTHING'S COMING UP ROSES

Excerpt

from *Gypsy*

Words by STEPHEN SONDHEIM
Music by JULE STYNE

For the complete song see: HL00740123 *The Singer's Musical Theatre Anthology, Mezzo-Soprano/Belter Vol. 3,* and other sources.

FLAMING AGNES
from *I Do! I Do!*

Words by TOM JONES
Music by HARVEY SCHMIDT

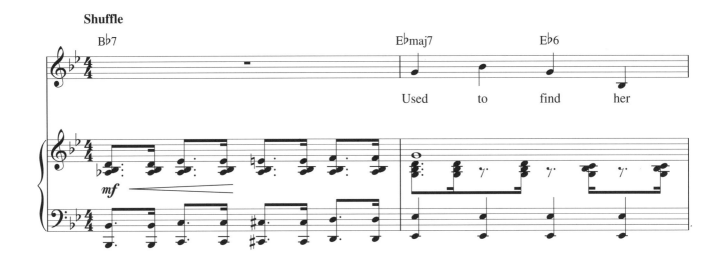

For the complete song see: HL00312208 *I Do! I Do!* vocal score.

GOD HELP THE OUTCASTS

from *Walt Disney's The Hunchback of Notre Dame*

Music by ALAN MENKEN
Lyrics by STEPHEN SCHWARTZ

For the complete song see: HL00313045 *The Hunchback of Notre Dame* vocal selections, and other sources.

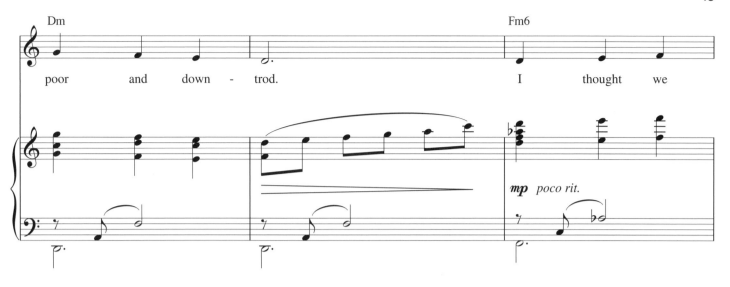

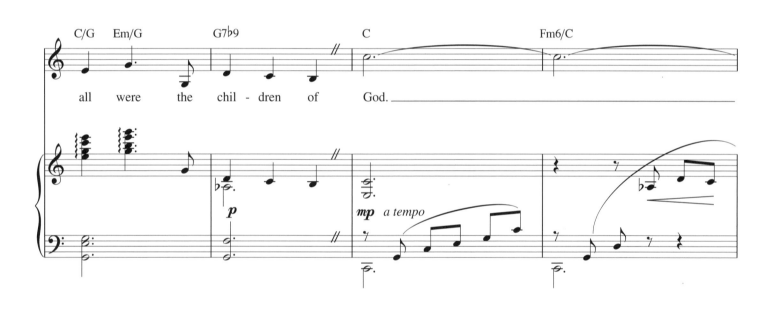

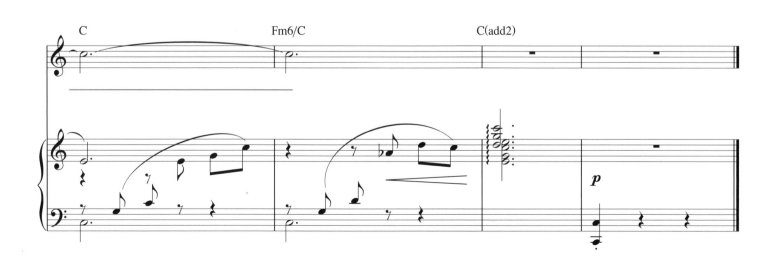

Excerpt

GOTTA HAVE ME GO WITH YOU

from the Motion Picture *A Star is Born*

Lyric by IRA GERSHWIN
Music by HAROLD ARLEN

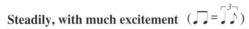

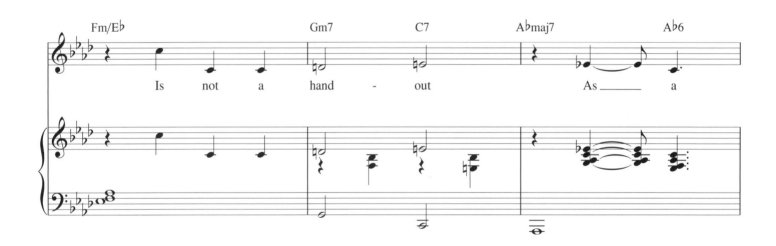

For the complete song see: HL00384828 *A Star Is Born* vocal selections.

HAPPY TO KEEP HIS DINNER WARM

Excerpt

from *How to Succeed in Business Without Really Trying*

By FRANK LOESSER

For the complete song see: HL00361072 *The Singer's Musical Theatre Anthology, Mezzo-Soprano/Belter Vol. 1 (Revised),* and other sources.

HIT ME WITH A HOT NOTE
from *Sophisticated Ladies*

Words and Music by DUKE ELLINGTON
and DON GEORGE

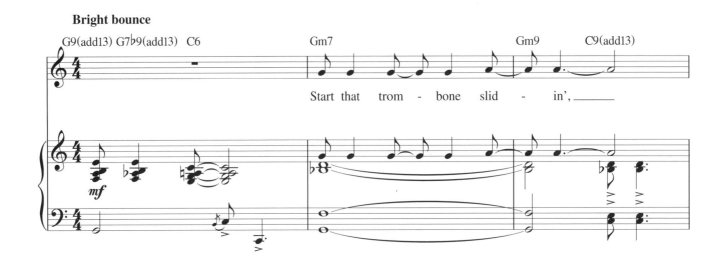

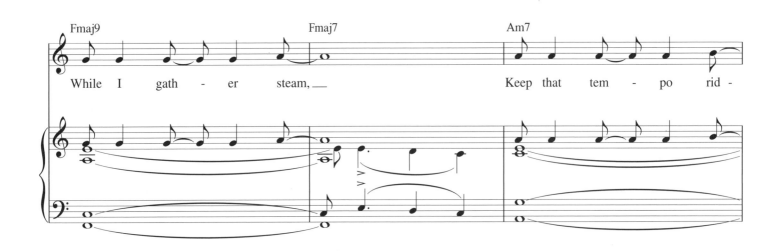

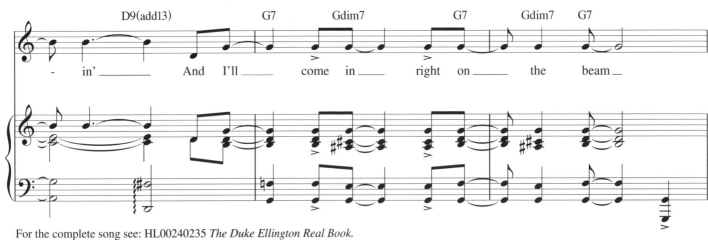

For the complete song see: HL00240235 *The Duke Ellington Real Book.*

HOLDING OUT FOR A HERO
from the Broadway Musical *Footloose*

Words by DEAN PITCHFORD
Music by JIM STEINMAN

Disco Appassionata

For the complete song see: HL00313133 *Footloose* Broadway vocal selections, and other sources.

Excerpt

HONEY BUN
from *South Pacific*

Lyrics by OSCAR HAMMERSTEIN II
Music by RICHARD RODGERS

Allegretto

She's my ba - by, I'm her pap! —

I'm her boo - by, she's my trap! — I am caught and

don't want - a run ___ 'Cause I'm hav - in' so much fun with Hon - ey

For the complete song see: HL00740123 *The Singer's Musical Theatre Anthology, Mezzo-Soprano/Belter Vol. 3,* and other sources.

THE HOSTESS WITH THE MOSTES' ON THE BALL

Excerpt

from the Stage Production *Call Me Madam*

Words and Music by
IRVING BERLIN

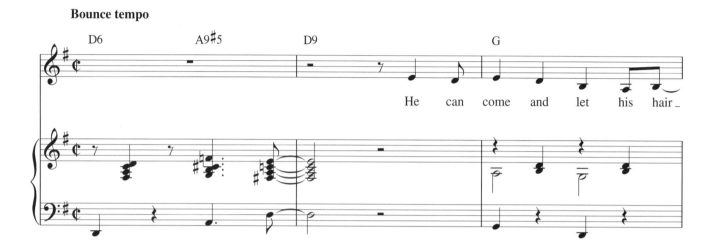

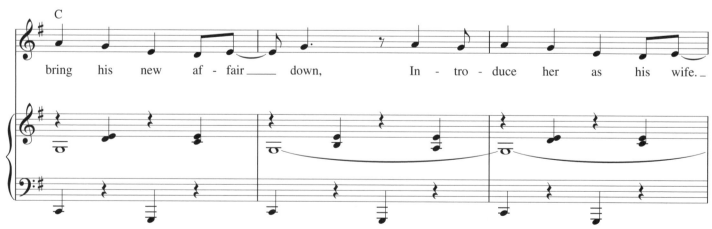

For the complete song see: HL00361072 *The Singer's Musical Theatre Anthology, Mezzo-Soprano/Belter Vol. 1 (Revised)*, and other sources.

Excerpt

HOW CAN I WAIT?
from *Paint Your Wagon*

Words by ALAN JAY LERNER
Music by FREDERICK LOEWE

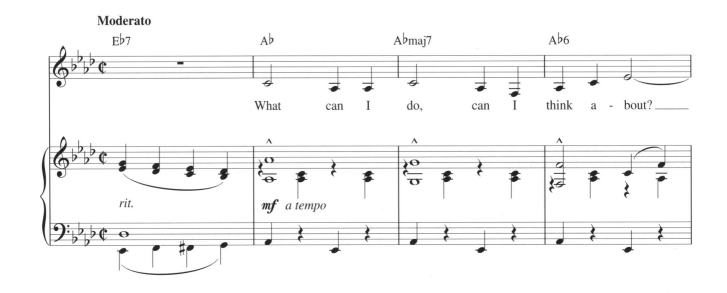

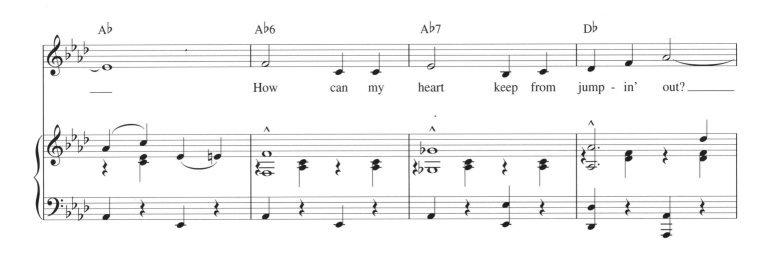

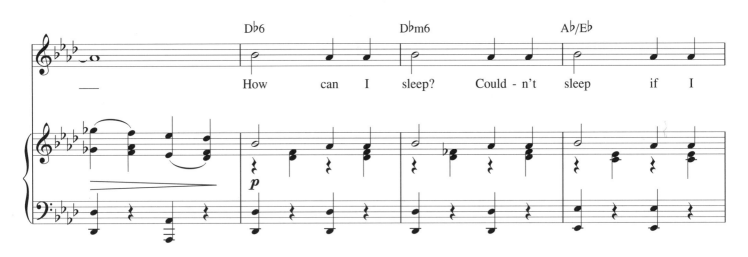

Excerpt

HOW DID WE COME TO THIS?

from *The Wild Party*

Words and Music by
ANDREW LIPPA

For the complete song see: HL00313162 *The Wild Party* vocal selections.

Excerpt

I AIN'T DOWN YET
from *The Unsinkable Molly Brown*

By MEREDITH WILLSON

For the complete song see: HL00361072 *The Singer's Musical Theatre Anthology, Mezzo-Soprano/Belter Vol. 1 (Revised)*, and other sources.

HOW I FEEL
from *The Me Nobody Knows*

Words by WILL HOLT
Music by GARY FRIEDMAN

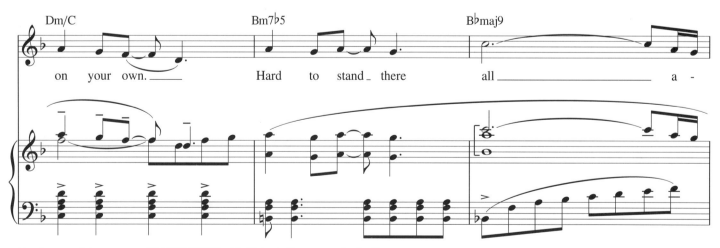

For the complete song see: HL00360472 *The Me Nobody Knows* vocal selections.

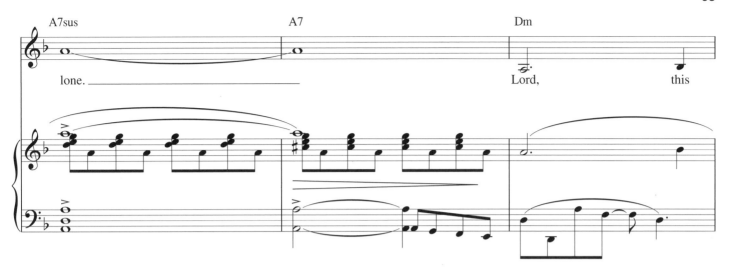

lone. _____ Lord, this

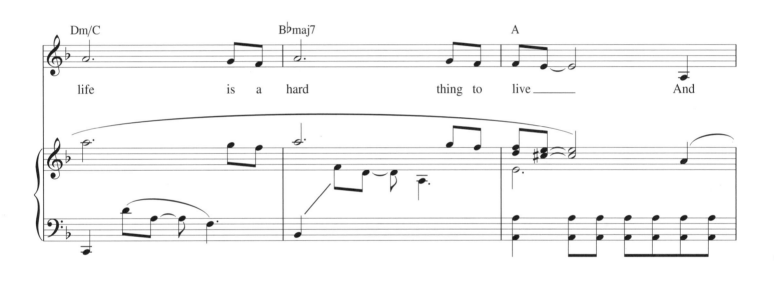

life is a hard thing to live _____ And

hard - er still to leave. _____

HURRY IT'S LOVELY UP HERE
from *On A Clear Day You Can See Forever*

Words by ALAN JAY LERNER
Music by BURTON LANE

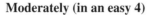

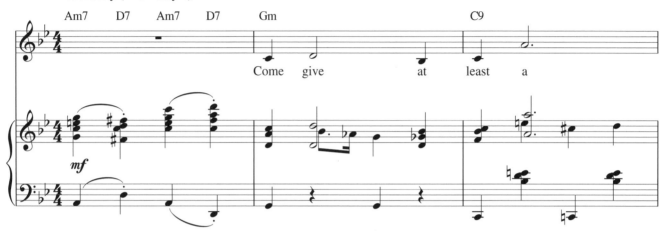

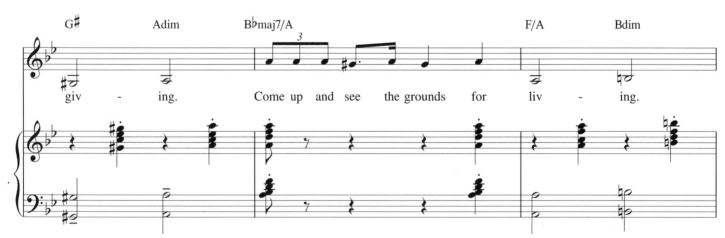

For the complete song see: HL00312297 *On a Clear Day You Can See Forever* vocal selections.

Stronger 4

Come poke your head out. ___ O - pen up and

spread out. ___ Hur - ry, it's love - ly

here. ___

I (WHO HAVE NOTHING)
from *Smokey Joe's Cafe*

English language lyric by JERRY LEIBER and MIKE STOLLER
Original Italian lyric by MOGOL
Music by CARLO DONIDA

For the complete song see: HL00313080 *Smokey Joe's Cafe* vocal selections.

I CAIN'T SAY NO
from *Oklahoma!*

Lyrics by OSCAR HAMMERSTEIN II
Music by RICHARD RODGERS

Brightly (in 2)

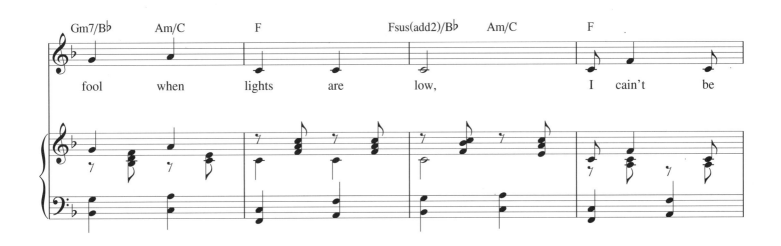

For the complete song see: HL00361072 *The Singer's Musical Theatre Anthology, Mezzo-Soprano/Belter Vol. 1 (Revised)*, and other sources.

I DREAMED A DREAM
from *Les Misérables*

Music by CLAUDE-MICHEL SCHÖNBERG
Lyrics by ALAIN BOUBIL,
JEAN-MARC NATEL and HERBERT KRETZMER

For the complete song see: HL00747031 *The Singer's Musical Theatre Anthology, Mezzo-Soprano/Belter Vol. 2 (Revised),* and other sources.

Excerpt

I ENJOY BEING A GIRL
from *Flower Drum Song*

Lyrics by OSCAR HAMMERSTEIN II
Music by RICHARD RODGERS

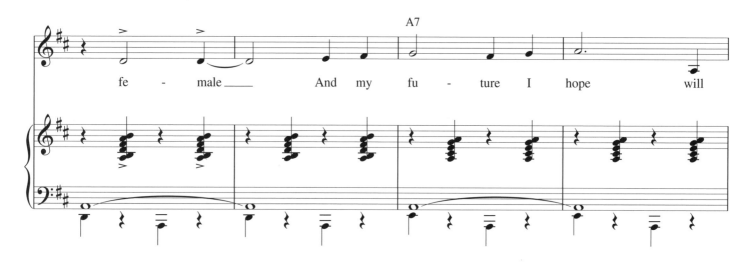

For the complete song see: HL00361072 *The Singer's Musical Theatre Anthology, Mezzo-Soprano/Belter Vol. 1 (Revised)*, and other sources.

I GOT THE SUN IN THE MORNING

Excerpt

from the Stage Production *Annie Get Your Gun*

Words and Music by
IRVING BERLIN

Medium Jump Tempo

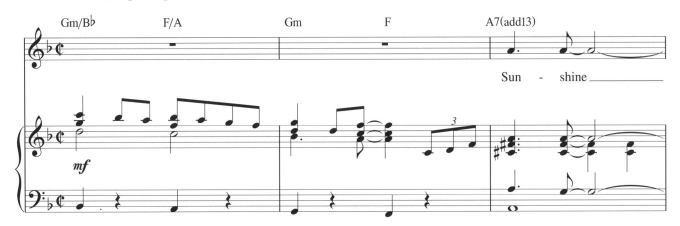

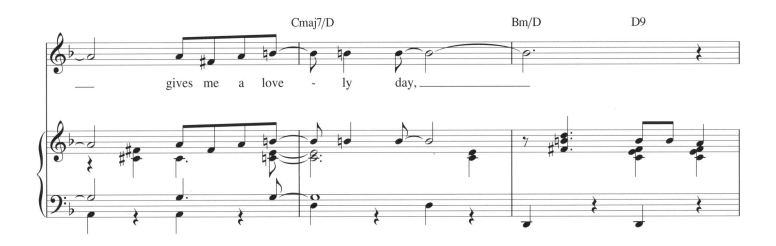

For the complete song see: HL00361072 *The Singer's Musical Theatre Anthology, Mezzo-Soprano/Belter Vol. 1 (Revised),* and other sources.

Excerpt

I KNOW THE TRUTH
from Walt Disney Theatrical Productions' *Aida*

Music by ELTON JOHN
Lyrics by TIM RICE

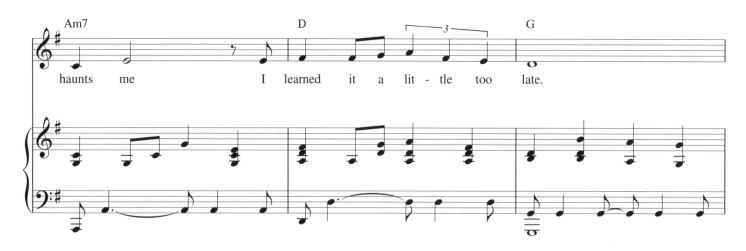

For the complete song see: HL00313175 *Aida* vocal selections.

I LOVE A PIANO

from the Stage Production *Stop! Look! Listen!*

Words and Music by
IRVING BERLIN

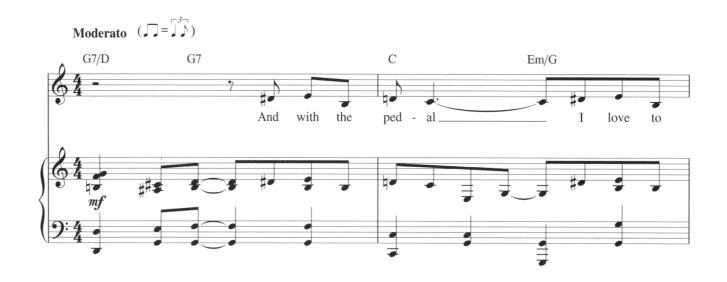

And with the ped - al _____ I love to

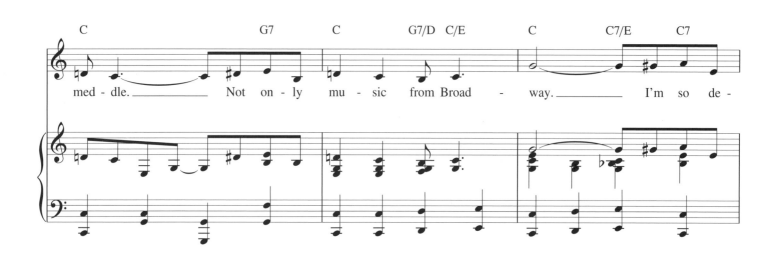

med - dle. _____ Not on - ly mu - sic from Broad - way. _____ I'm so de -

light - ed _____ if I'm in - vit - ed _____ to hear a

For the complete song see: HL000050089*I Love a Piano* piano/vocal sheet music, and other sources.

Excerpt

I WANT TO BE BAD
from *Good News*

Words and Music by B.G. DeSYLVA,
LEW BROWN and RAY HENDERSON

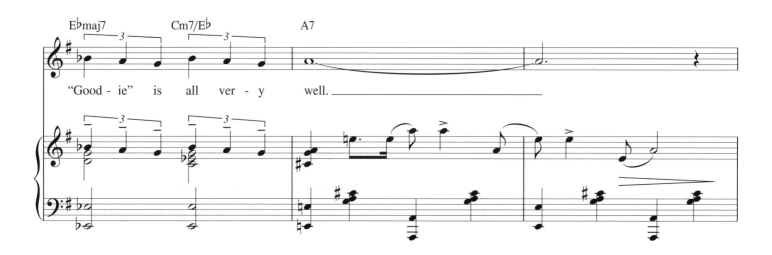

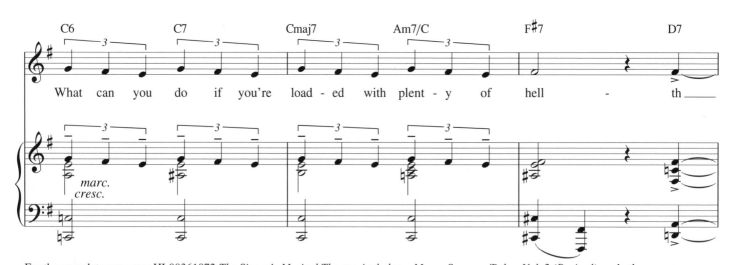

For the complete song see: HL00361072 *The Singer's Musical Theatre Anthology, Mezzo-Soprano/Belter Vol. 2 (Revised),* and other sources.

and vi - gor? When you're learn - ing what lips are for ___

If it's naught - y to ask for more ___ Let a lad - y con -

fess I want ___ to be bad. ___

I'M BEGINNING TO SEE THE LIGHT

Excerpt

featured in *Sophisticated Ladies*

Words and Music by DON GEORGE, JOHNNY HODGES,
DUKE ELLINGTON and HARRY JAMES

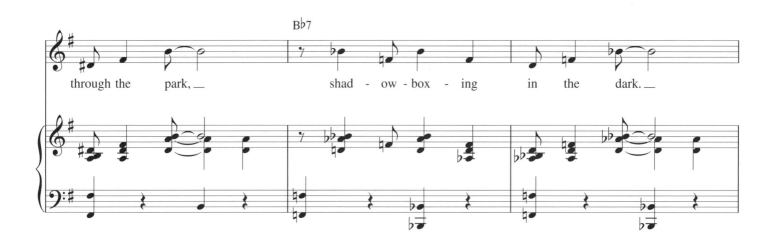

For the complete song see: HL00304086 *I'm Beginning to See the Light* piano/vocal sheet music, and other sources.

I nev-er made love by lan-tern shine,___ I

nev-er saw rain-bows in my wine,___ but now that your lips are

burn-ing mine,___ I'm be-gin-ning to see the light.___

8vb

I'M GOING BACK
from *Bells Are Ringing*

Words by BETTY COMDEN
and ADOLPH GREEN
Music by JULE STYNE

For the complete song see: HL00311608 *Broadway Belter's Songbook.*

IF HE WALKED INTO MY LIFE
from *Mame*

Music and Lyric by
JERRY HERMAN

Were the years a lit-tle fast? _____ Was his world a lit-tle free? _____ Was there too much of a crowd, All too lush and loud And not e-nough of me? Tho' I'll ask my-self my

For the complete song see: HL00747031 *The Singer's Musical Theatre Anthology, Mezzo-Soprano/Belter Vol. 2 (Revised),* and other sources.

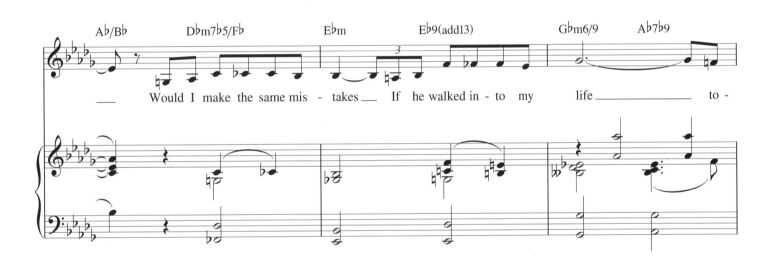

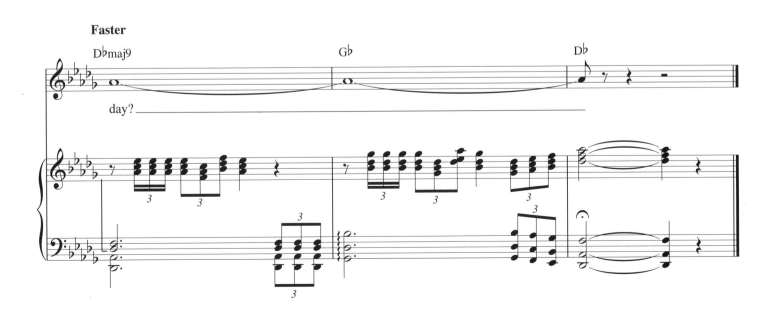

Excerpt

IF I CAN'T HAVE YOU
from the Motion Picture *Saturday Night Fever*

Words and Music by ROBIN GIBB,
MAURICE GIBB and BARRY GIBB

Medium rock beat

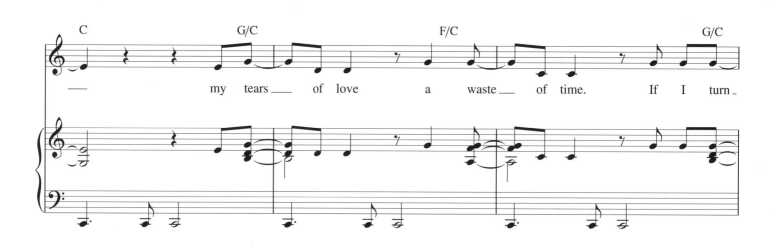

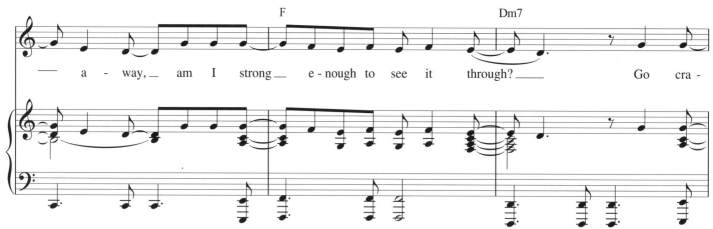

For the complete song see: HL00313160 *Saturday Night Fever* vocal selections, and other sources.

Excerpt

IF I WERE A BELL
from *Guys and Dolls*

By FRANK LOESSER

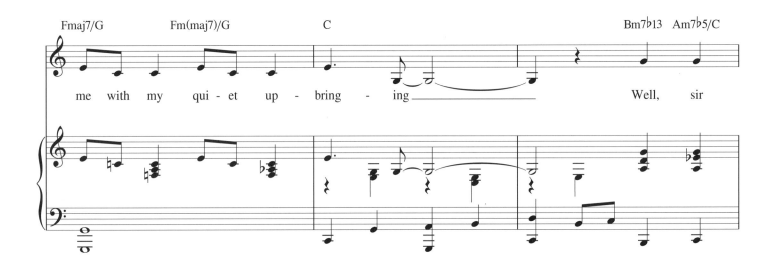

For the complete song see: HL00446425 *Guys and Dolls* vocal selections, and other sources.

IF YOU REALLY KNEW ME
from *They're Playing Our Song*

Words by CAROLE BAYER SAGER
Music by MARVIN HAMLISCH

For the complete song see: HL00747031 *The Singer's Musical Theatre Anthology, Mezzo-Soprano/Belter Vol. 2 (Revised),* and other sources.

IT'S A PERFECT RELATIONSHIP

Excerpt

from *Bells Are Ringing*

Words by BETTY COMDEN
and ADOLPH GREEN
Music by JULE STYNE

For the complete song see: HL00747035 *The Actor's Songbook, Women's Edition.*

Excerpt

IT'S MY PARTY

Words and Music by HERB WIENER,
WALLY GOLD and JOHN GLUCK, JR.

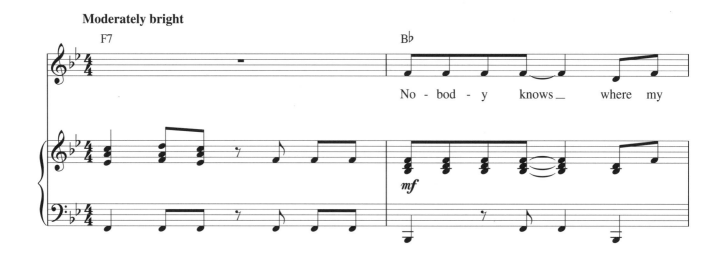

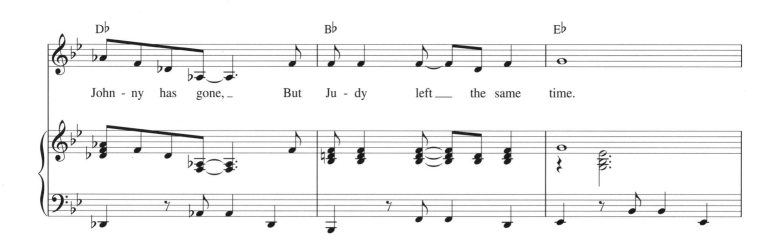

For the complete song see: HL00310127 *My Boyfriend's Back (folio)*, and other sources.

Excerpt

IT'S TODAY
from *Mame*

Music and Lyric by
JERRY HERMAN

For the complete song see: HL00384226 *Mame* vocal selections, and other sources.

JACOB AND SONS
from *Joseph and the Amazing Technicolor Dreamcoat*

Music by ANDREW LLOYD WEBBER
Lyrics by TIM RICE

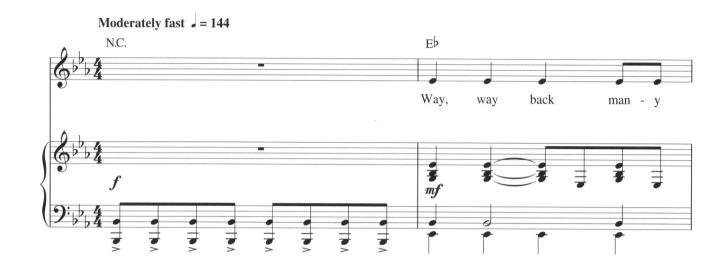

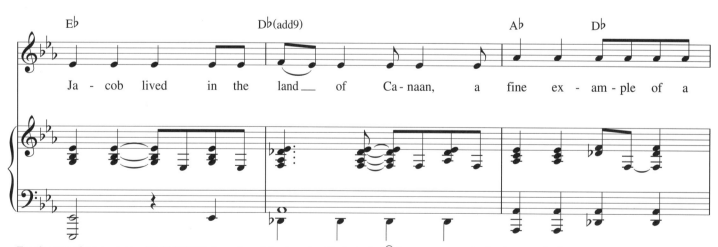

For the complete song see: HL00312505 *Joseph and the Amazing Technicolor ®Dreamcoat* vocal selections, and other sources.

Excerpt

JOHNNY ONE NOTE
from *Babes in Arms*

Words by LORENZ HART
Music by RICHARD RODGERS

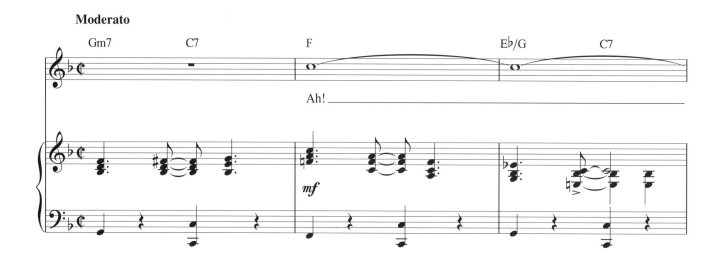

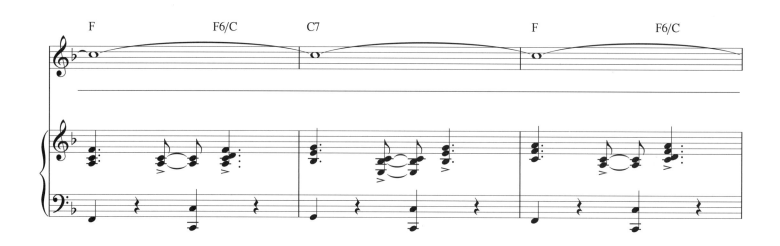

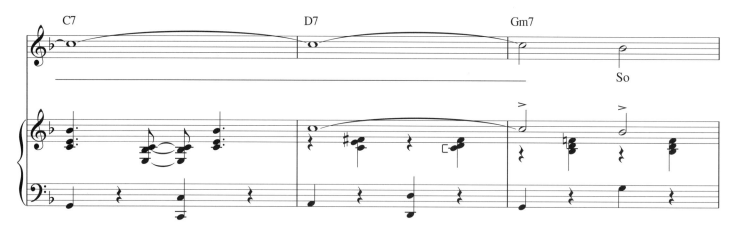

For the complete song see: HL00747031 *The Singer's Musical Theatre Anthology, Mezzo-Soprano/Belter Vol. 2 (Revised)*, and other sources.

KEEPIN' OUT OF MISCHIEF NOW

Excerpt

featured in *Ain't Misbehavin'*

Lyric by ANDY RAZAF
Music by THOMAS "FATS" WALLER

Moderately slow

So, I'm keep - in' out of mis - chief

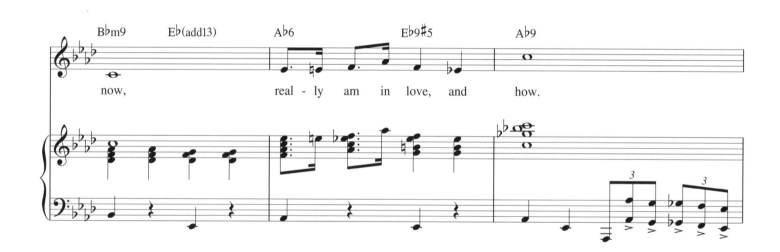

now, real - ly am in love, and how.

I have told them in ad - vance, __ they can't break up

For the complete song see: HL00359040 *Ain't Misbehavin'* vocal selections.

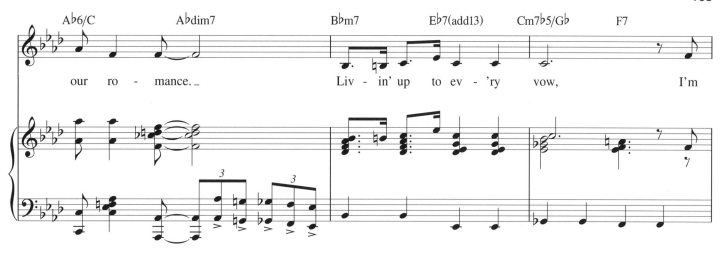

our ro - mance.___ Liv - in' up to ev - 'ry vow, I'm

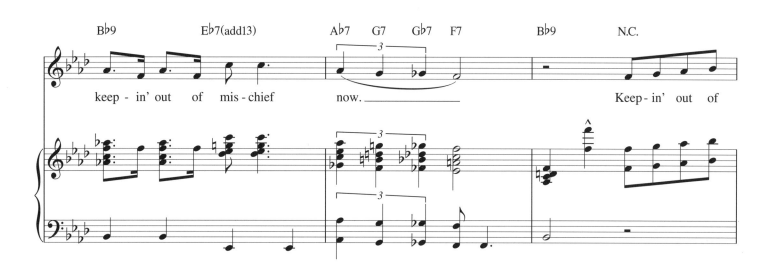

keep - in' out of mis - chief now._____ Keep - in' out of

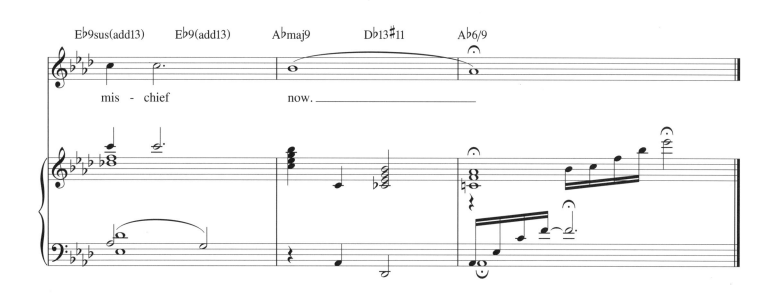

mis - chief now._____

LET YOURSELF GO
from the Motion Picture *Follow the Fleet*

Words and Music by
IRVING BERLIN

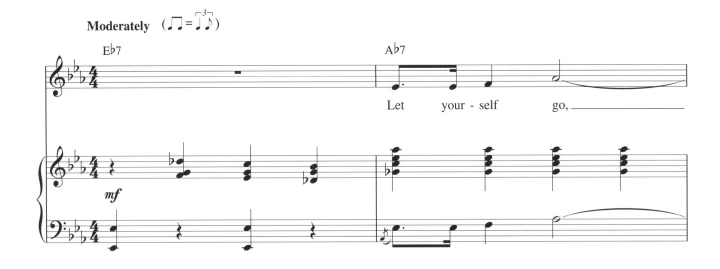

For the complete song see: HL00005138 *Let Yourself Go* piano/vocal sheet, and other sources.

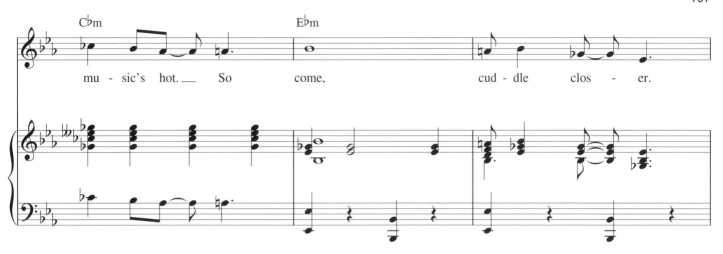

mu - sic's hot.___ So come, cud - dle clos - er.

Don't you dare to an - swer, "No ___ Sir." Butch - er, bank - er,

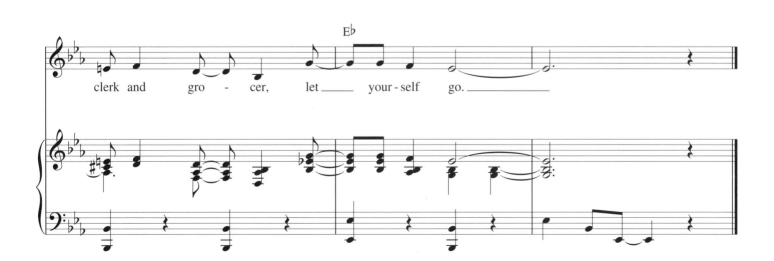

clerk and gro - cer, let ___ your - self go. ___

LET'S HEAR IT FOR THE BOY
from the Broadway Musical *Footloose*

Words by DEAN PITCHFORD
Music by TOM SNOW

For the complete song see: HL00313133 *Footloose* Broadway vocal selections, and other sources.

LOADS OF LOVE
from *No Strings*

Lyrics and Music by
RICHARD RODGERS

For the complete song see: HL00312280 *No Strings* vocal selections.

Excerpt

LOOK AT THAT FACE

from *The Roar of the Greasepaint – The Smell of the Crowd*

Words and Music by LESLIE BRICUSSE
and ANTHONY NEWLEY

For the complete song see: HL00313156 *The Roar of the Greasepaint – The Smell of the Crowd* vocal selections.

LOOK WHAT HAPPENED TO MABEL

from the Musical *Mack and Mabel*

Music and Lyric by
JERRY HERMAN

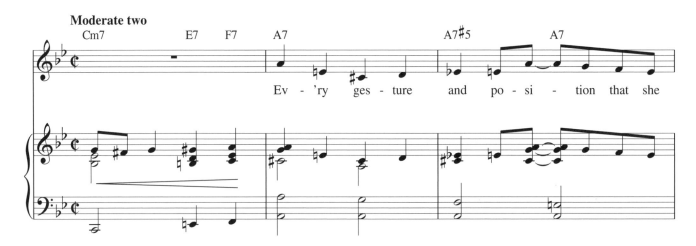

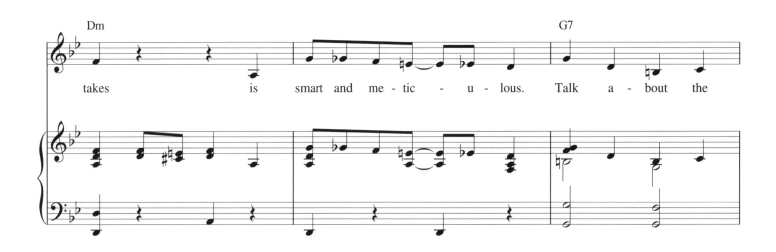

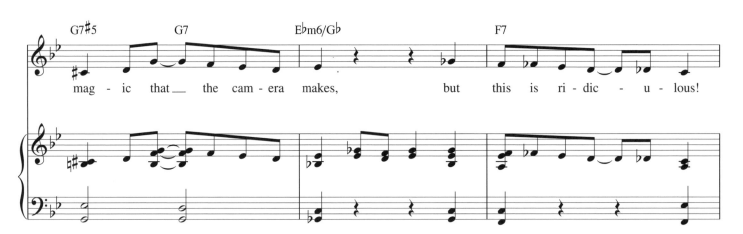

For the complete song see: HL00384205 *Mack and Mabel* vocal selections.

LOSING MY MIND
from *Follies*

Words and Music by
STEPHEN SONDHEIM

For the complete song see: HL00361072 *The Singer's Musical Theatre Anthology, Mezzo-Soprano/Belter Vol. 1 (Revised)*, and other sources.

A LOT OF LIVIN' TO DO
from *Bye Bye Birdie*

Lyric by LEE ADAMS
Music by CHARLES STROUSE

For the complete song see: HL00313233 *Bye Bye Birdie* vocal selections, and other sources.

MAYBE THIS TIME
from the Musical *Cabaret*

Words by FRED EBB
Music by JOHN KANDER

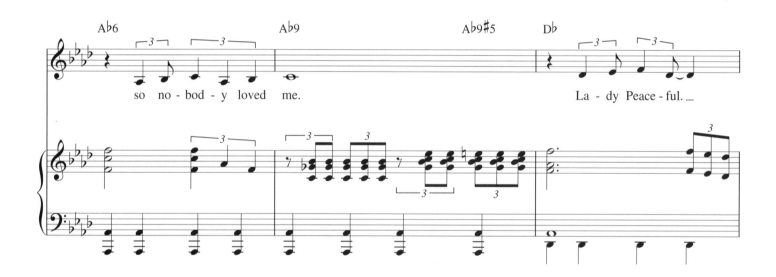

For the complete song see: HL00740123 *The Singer's Musical Theatre Anthology, Mezzo-Soprano/Belter Vol. 3 (Revised)*, and other sources.

MEAN TO ME
from *Ain't Misbehavin'*

Lyric and Music by FRED E. AHLERT
and ROY TURK

For the complete song see: HL00353252 *Mean to Me* piano/vocal sheet music, and other sources.

MY GUY

Excerpt

Words and Music by
WILLIAM "SMOKEY" ROBINSON

For the complete song see: HL00310367 *The Motown Anthology,* and other sources.

THE MUSIC THAT MAKES ME DANCE

from *Funny Girl*

Words by BOB MERRILL
Music by JULE STYNE

For the complete song see: HL00747031 *The Singer's Musical Theatre Anthology, Mezzo-Soprano/Belter Vol. 2 (Revised),* and other sources.

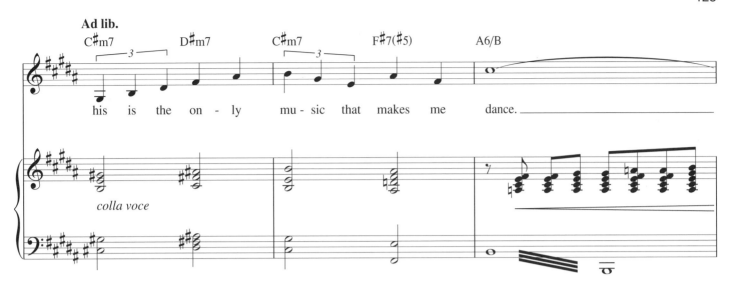

Ad lib.

C#m7 D#m7 C#m7 F#7(#5) A6/B

his is the on - ly mu - sic that makes me dance.____

colla voce

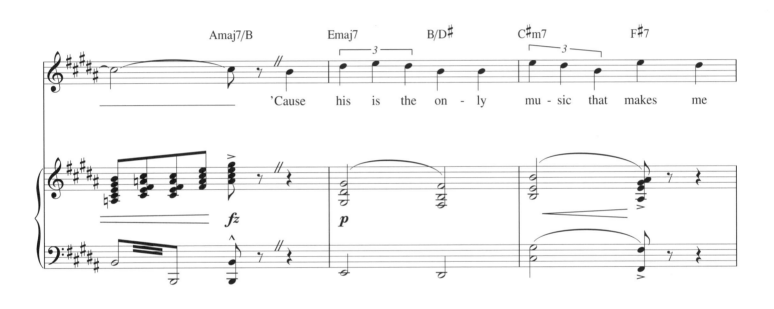

Amaj7/B Emaj7 B/D# C#m7 F#7

____ 'Cause his is the on - ly mu - sic that makes me

fz *p*

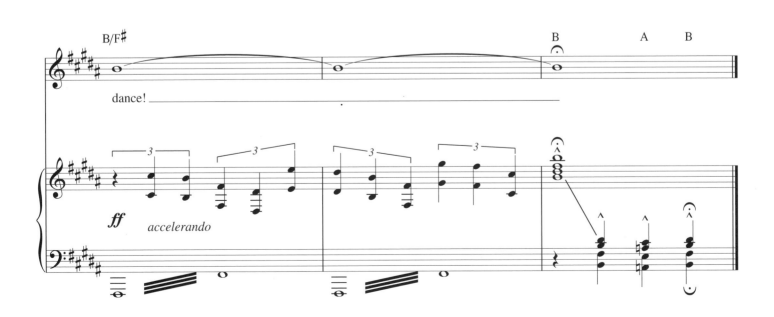

B/F# B A B

dance!____

ff *accelerando*

NOBODY'S CHASING ME

from *Out of This World*

Words and Music by
COLE PORTER

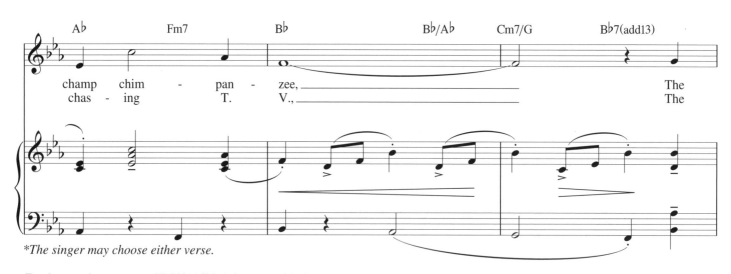

*The singer may choose either verse.

For the complete song see: HL00311627 *Cole Porter: 22 Clever & Funny Songs,* and other sources.

NOW THAT I'VE SEEN HER
from *Miss Saigon*

Music by CLAUDE-MICHEL SCHÖNBERG
Lyrics by RICHARD MALTBY JR. and ALAIN BOUBLIL
Adapted from original French Lyrics by ALAIN BOUBLIL

For the complete song see: HL00490405 *Miss Saigon* vocal selections, and other sources.

Excerpt

ONE HALLOWE'EN
from the Broadway Musical *Applause*

Lyric by LEE ADAMS
Music by CHARLES STROUSE

For the complete song see: HL00313231 *Applause* vocal and other sources.

N.Y.C.
from the Musical Production *Annie*

Lyric by MARTIN CHARNIN
Music by CHARLES STROUSE

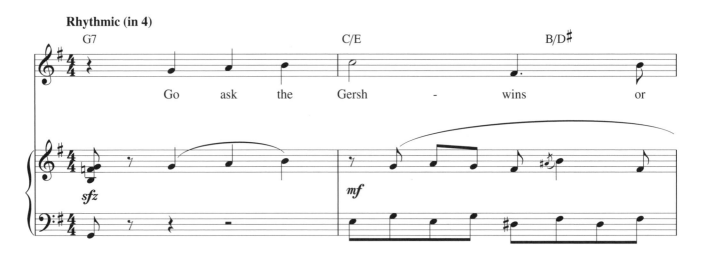

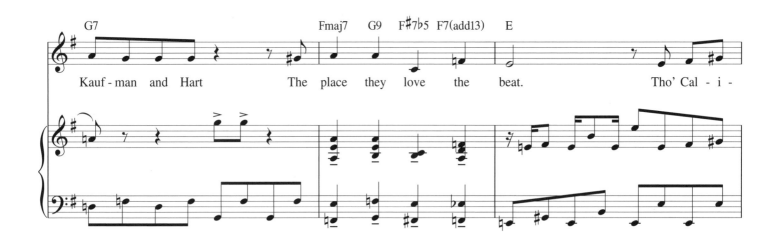

For the complete song see: HL00381600 *N.Y.C* piano/vocal sheet music, and other sources.

OH, YOU WONDERFUL BOY

from *George M!*

Words and Music by
GEORGE M. COHAN

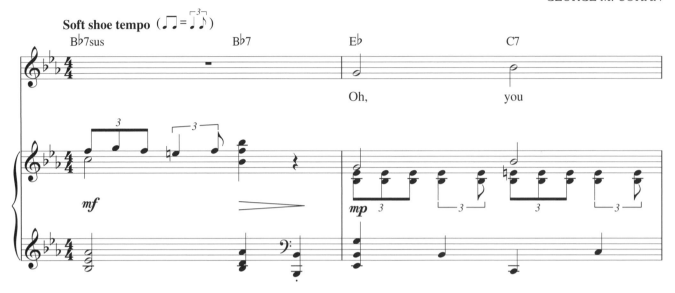

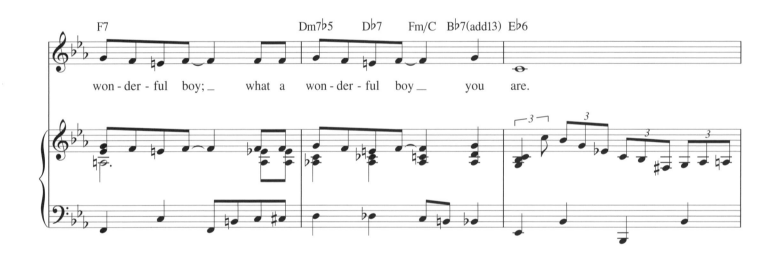

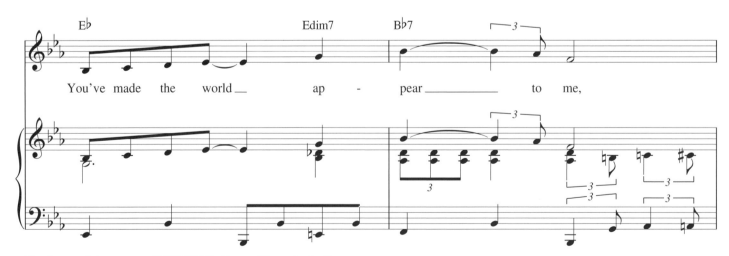

For the complete song see: HL00008203 *George M!* vocal selections.

Excerpt

ON MY OWN
from *Les Misérables*

Music by CLAUDE-MICHEL SCHÖNBERG
Lyrics by ALAIN BOUBLIL, JOHN CAIRD,
TREVOR NUNN, JEAN-MARC NATEL
and HERBERT KRETZMER

For the complete song see: HL00747031 *The Singer's Musical Theatre Anthology, Mezzo-Soprano/Belter Vol. 2 (Revised),* and other sources.

ONE FINE DAY

Words and Music by GERRY GOFFIN
and CAROLE KING

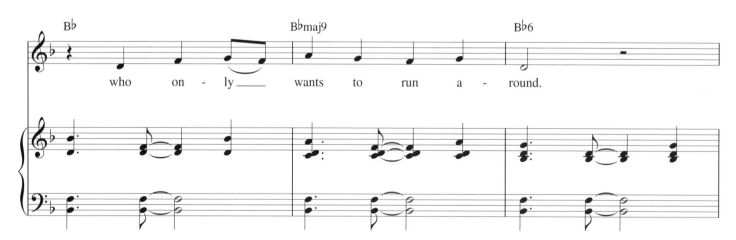

For the complete song see: HL00310127 *My Boyfriend's Back* (folio), and other sources.

OOH! MY FEET!

from *The Most Happy Fella*

Words and Music by
FRANK LOESSER

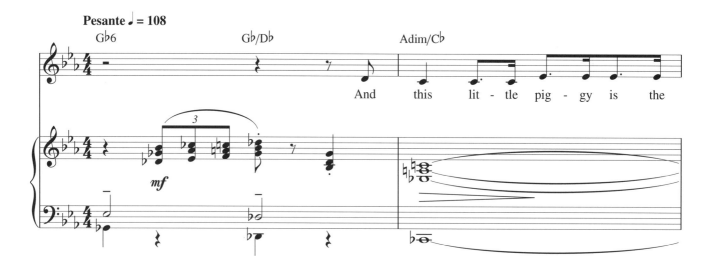

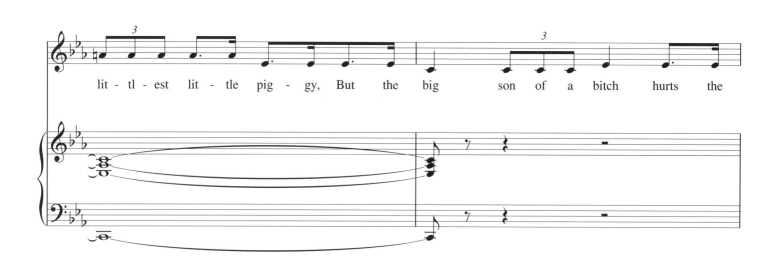

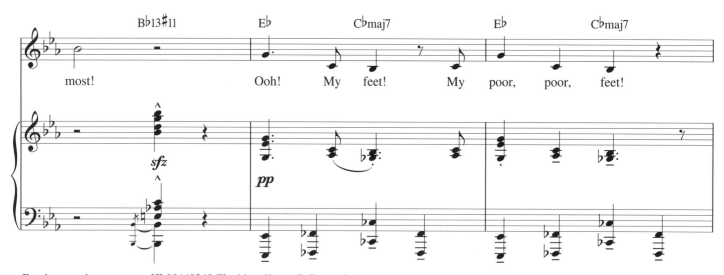

For the complete song see: HL00448248 *The Most Happy Fella* vocal score.

PLANT YOU NOW, DIG YOU LATER

Excerpt

from *Pal Joey*

Words by LORENZ HART
Music by RICHARD RODGERS

For the complete song see: HL00312314 *Pal Joey* vocal score.

Excerpt

REFLECTION
from Walt Disney Pictures' *Mulan*

Music by MATTHEW WILDER
Lyrics by DAVID ZIPPEL

For the complete song see: HL00313099 *Mulan* vocal selections, and other sources.

Excerpt

A QUIET THING
from *Flora, the Red Menace*

Lyrics by FRED EBB
Music by JOHN KANDER

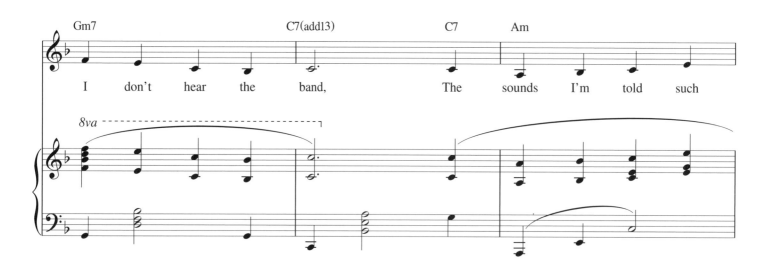

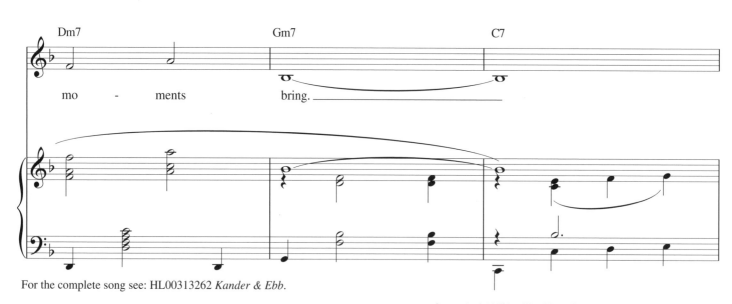

For the complete song see: HL00313262 *Kander & Ebb.*

SARA LEE

Words by FRED EBB
Music by JOHN KANDER

With a bounce

And that's o - kay by me.

Broad cakewalk

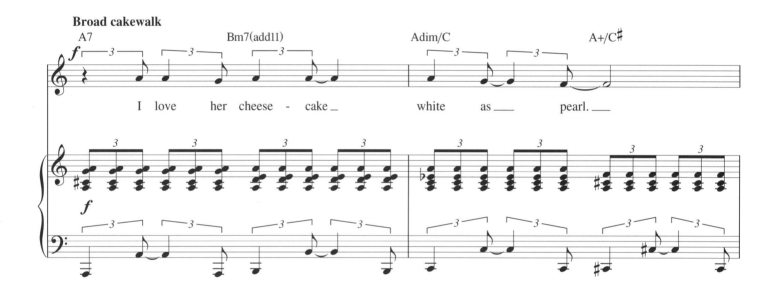

I love her cheese - cake _ white as _ pearl. _

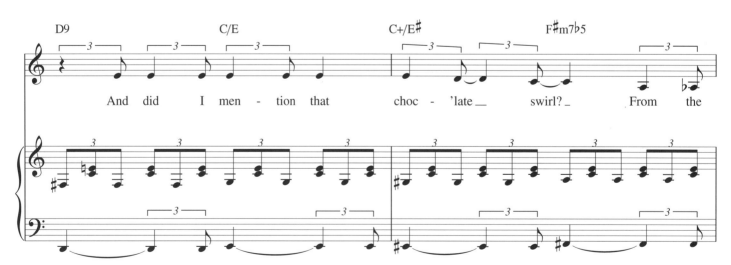

And did I men - tion that choc - 'late _ swirl? _ From the

For the complete song see: HL00310239 *Contemporary Cabaret*.

Excerpt

SHAKING THE BLUES AWAY
from the Motion Picture Irving Berlin's *Easter Parade*

Words and Music by
IRVING BERLIN

For the complete song see: HL00005221 *Shaking the Blues Away* piano/vocal sheet music, and other sources.

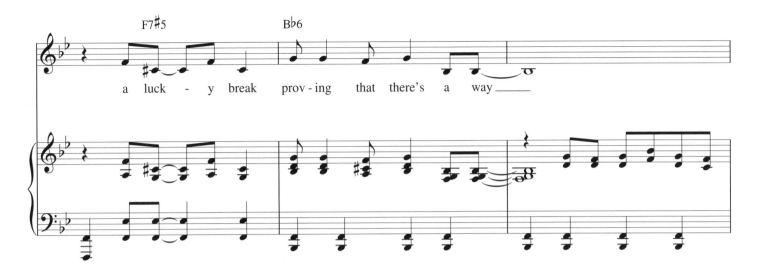

a luck - y break prov - ing that there's a way ____

to chase your cares a - way. ____ If you would lose your wear -

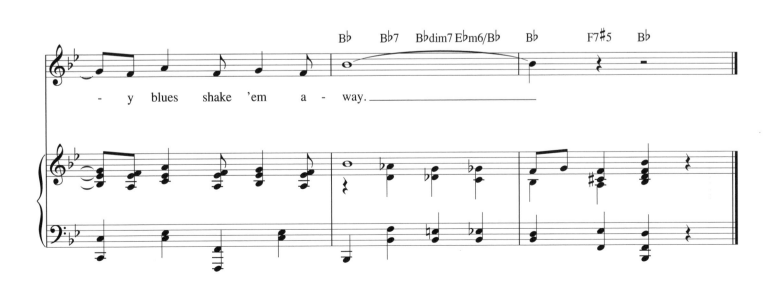

- y blues shake 'em a - way. ____

Excerpt

SHY
from *Once Upon a Mattress*

Words by MARSHALL BARER
Music by MARY RODGERS

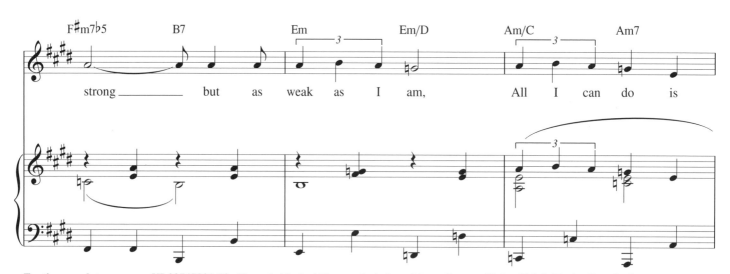

For the complete song see: HL00747031 *The Singer's Musical Theatre Anthology, Mezzo-Soprano/Belter Vol. 2 (Revised)*, and other sources.

Excerpt

SING HAPPY
from *Flora, the Red Menace*

Words by FRED EBB
Music by JOHN KANDER

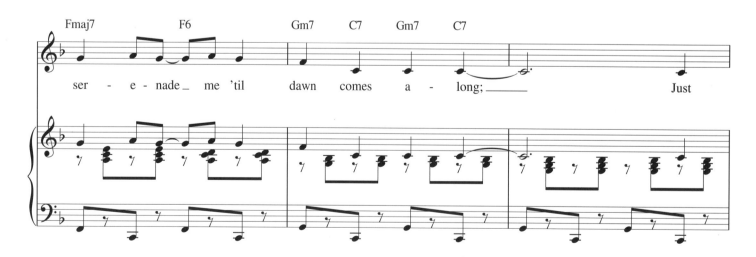

Excerpt

SO FAR AWAY

Words and Music by
CAROLE KING

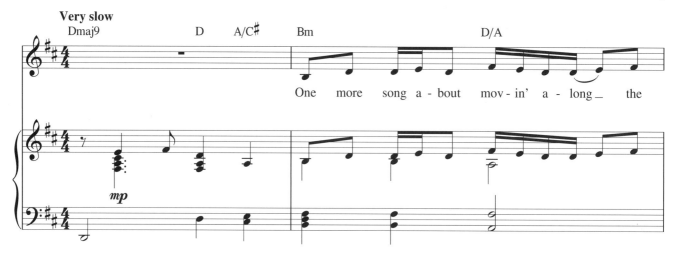

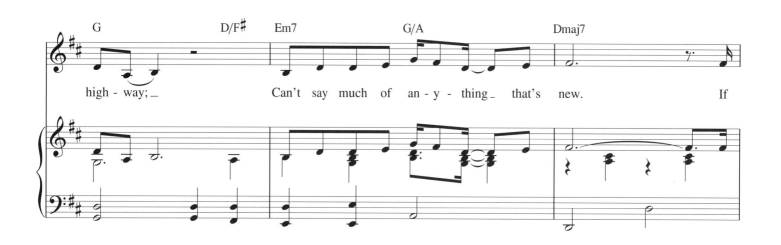

For the complete song see: HL00306090 *Carole King Deluxe,* and other sources.

SOME PEOPLE
from *Gypsy*

Words by STEPHEN SONDHEIM
Music by JULE STYNE

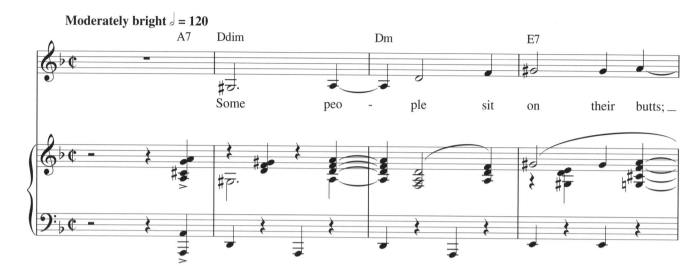

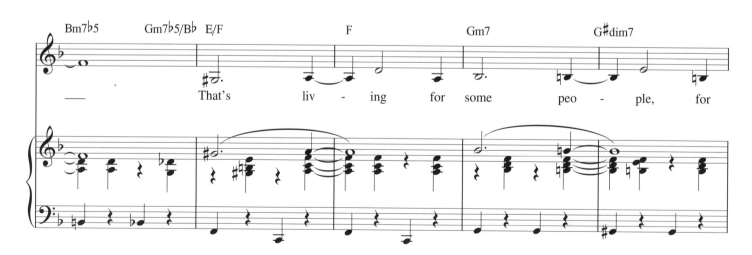

For the complete song see: HL00361072 *The Singer's Musical Theatre Anthology, Mezzo-Soprano/Belter Vol. 1 (Revised),* and other sources.

Excerpt

SOMEONE LIKE YOU
from *Jekyll & Hyde*

Words by LESLIE BRICUSSE
Music by FRANK WILDHORN

For the complete song see: HL00740123 *The Singer's Musical Theatre Anthology, Mezzo-Soprano/Belter Vol. 3,* and other sources.

SOMEONE WOKE UP

from *Do I Hear a Waltz?*

Music by RICHARD RODGERS
Lyrics by STEPHEN SONDHEIM

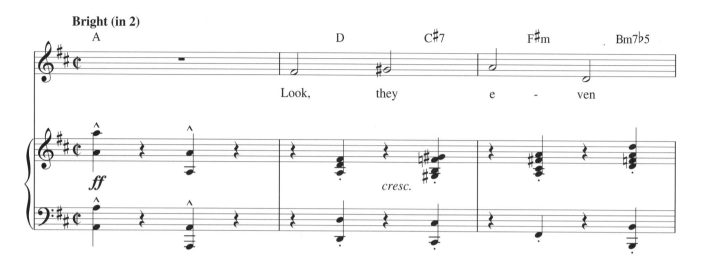

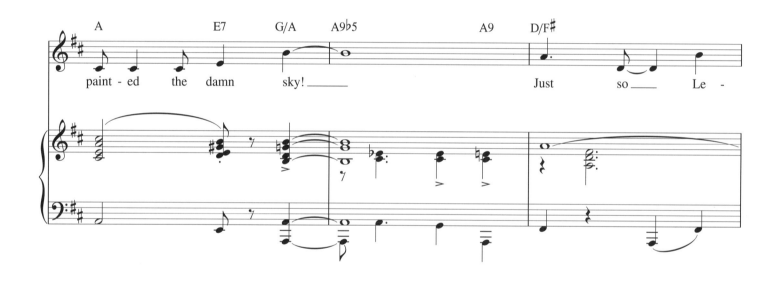

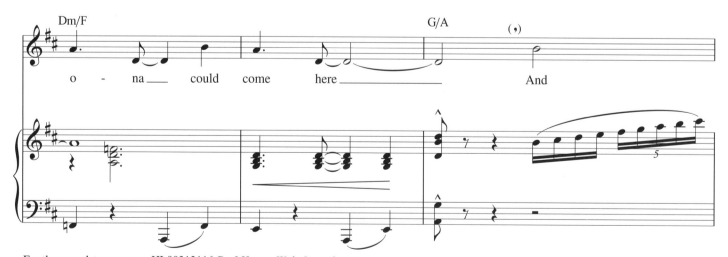

For the complete song see: HL00312116 *Do I Hear a Waltz?* vocal score.

Excerpt

TAKE ME OR LEAVE ME

from *Rent*

Words and Music by
JONATHAN LARSON

For the complete song see: HL00313069 *Rent* vocal selections.

TAKE THAT LOOK OFF YOUR FACE

Excerpt

from *Song and Dance*

Music by ANDREW LLOYD WEBBER
Lyrics by DON BLACK

For the complete song see: HL00361100 *Song and Dance* vocal selections.

TEN CENTS A DANCE
from *Simple Simon*

Words by LORENZ HART
Music by RICHARD RODGERS

For the complete song see: HL00740039 *Musical Theatre Classics, Mezzo-Soprano/Belter Vol. 2*, and other sources.

Excerpt

THAT TERRIFIC RAINBOW

from *Pal Joey*

Words by LORENZ HART
Music by RICHARD RODGERS

For the complete song see: HL00312314 *Pal Joey* vocal score.

THERE ARE WORSE THINGS I COULD DO
from *Grease*

Lyric and Music by WARREN CASEY
and JIM JACOBS

For the complete song see: HL00383675 *Grease* vocal selections, and other sources.

Excerpt

WHAT DID I EVER SEE IN HIM

from *Bye Bye Birdie*

Lyric by LEE ADAMS
Music by CHARLES STROUSE

For the complete song see: HL00313230 *Bye Bye Birdie* vocal score.

THERE WON'T BE TRUMPETS
from *Anyone Can Whistle*

Words and Music by
STEPHEN SONDHEIM

For the complete song see: HL00747031 *The Singer's Musical Theatre Anthology, Mezzo-Soprano/Belter Vol. 2 (Revised)*.

WHAT DID I HAVE THAT I DON'T HAVE?

from *On a Clear Day You Can See Forever*

Words by ALAN JAY LERNER
Music by BURTON LANE

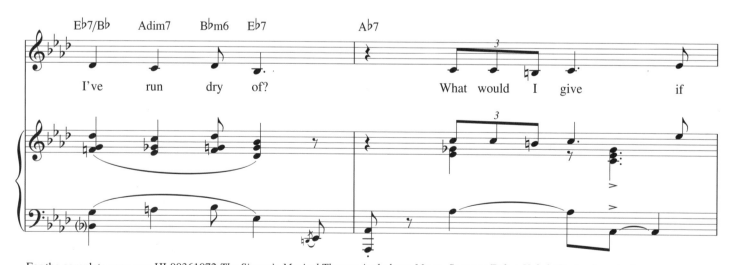

For the complete song see: HL00361072 *The Singer's Musical Theatre Anthology, Mezzo-Soprano/Belter Vol. 1 (Revised)*, and other sources.

my old know - how still knew how!

Oh!   What did I have I

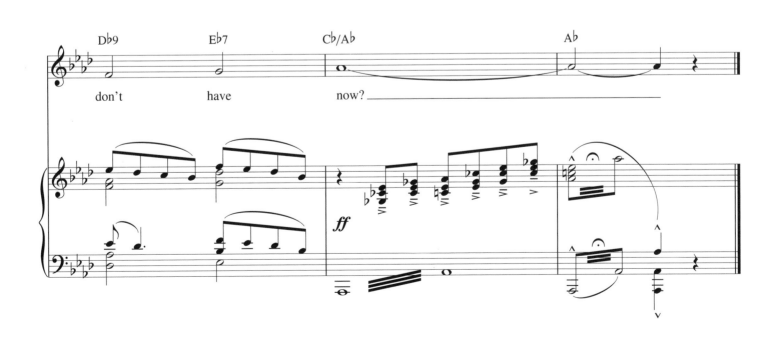

don't have now?

WHAT I DID FOR LOVE
from *A Chorus Line*

Music by MARVIN HAMLISCH
Lyric by EDWARD KLEBAN

For the complete song see: HL00747031 *The Singer's Musical Theatre Anthology, Mezzo-Soprano/Belter Vol. 2 (Revised),* and other sources.

Excerpt

WHAT MORE DO I NEED?

from *Saturday Night*

Music and Lyrics by
STEPHEN SONDHEIM

For the complete song see: HL00313107 *Saturday Night* vocal selections.

WHEN YOU'RE GOOD TO MAMA

Excerpt

from *Chicago*

Words by FRED EBB
Music by JOHN KANDER

Let's all stroke to - geth - er, ___ like the Prince-ton Crew. When you're strok - in' Ma-ma, ___ Ma - ma's strok - in' you. ___ So what's the one con - clu-sion I can bring this num - ber to? When you're good to Ma-ma, ___ Ma - ma's good to you. ___

For the complete song see: HL00740123 *The Singer's Musical Theatre Anthology, Mezzo-Soprano/Belter Vol. (Revised),* and other sources.

Excerpt

WHERE THE BOYS ARE
featured in the Motion Picture *Where the Boys Are*

Words and Music by HOWARD GREENFIELD
and NEIL SEDAKA

For the complete song see: HL00353374 *Where the Boys Are* piano/vocal sheet music, and other sources.

WILL YOU LOVE ME TOMORROW?
(Will You Still Love Me Tomorrow?)

Excerpt

Words and Music by GERRY GOFFIN
and CAROLE KING

For the complete song see: HL00308247 *Carole King: Tapestry,* and other sources.

WHEREVER HE AIN'T

from *Mack and Mabel*

Music and Lyric by
JERRY HERMAN

For the complete song see: HL00385217 *The Jerry Herman Songbook.*

A WONDERFUL GUY
from *South Pacific*

Lyrics by OSCAR HAMMERSTEIN II
Music by RICHARD RODGERS

For the complete song see: HL00361072 *The Singer's Musical Theatre Anthology, Mezzo-Soprano/Belter Vol. 1 (Revised),* and other sources.

Excerpt

YOU DON'T TELL ME
from *No Strings*

Lyrics and Music by
RICHARD RODGERS

For the complete song see: HL00312281 *No Strings* vocal score.

YOU CAN'T GET A MAN WITH A GUN

Excerpt

from the Stage Production *Annie Get Your Gun*

Words and Music by
IRVING BERLIN

For the complete song see: HL00740123 *The Singer's Musical Theatre Anthology, Mezzo-Soprano/Belter Vol. 3,* and other sources.

Excerpt

YOU'D BE SURPRISED
from *Ziegfeld Follies*

Words and Music by
IRVING BERLIN

He's such a del-i-cate thing but when he

starts in to squeeze, you'd be sur-prised. He does-n't

look ver-y strong but when you sit on his knees,

For the complete song see: HL00308088 *Irving Berlin – Novelty Songs,* and other sources.

YOU'D BETTER LOVE ME
from *High Spirits*

Words and Music by HUGH MARTIN
and TIMOTHY GRAY

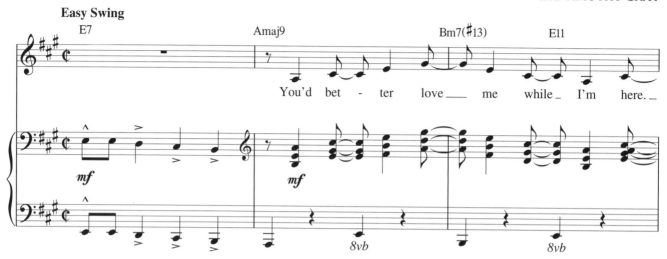

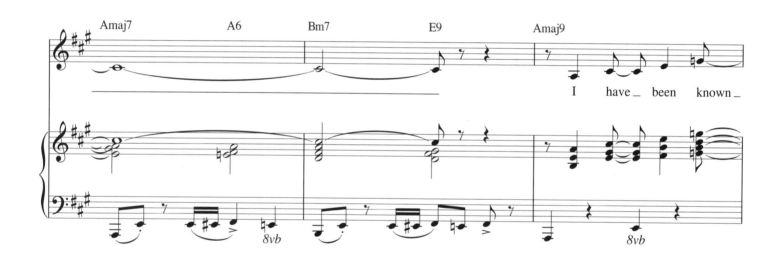

For the complete song see: HL00240046 *Ultimate Broadway Fake Book, 4th Edition.*

YOU'VE GOT POSSIBILITIES
from *"It's A Bird...It's A Plane...It's Superman"*

Lyric by LEE ADAMS
Music by CHARLES STROUSE

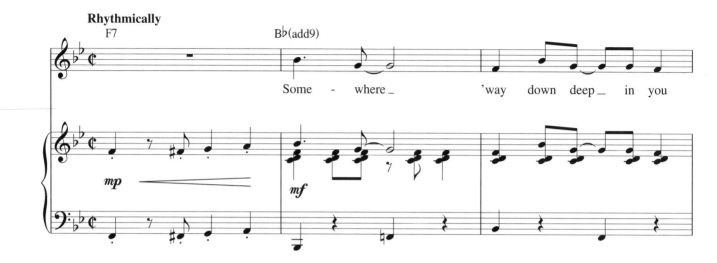

For the complete song see: HL00313247 *Songs of Charles Strouse.*

Excerpt

(I Wonder Why?)
YOU'RE JUST IN LOVE
from the Stage Production *Call Me Madam*

Words and Music by
IRVING BERLIN

For the complete song see: HL00005577 *Call Me Madam* vocal selections, and other sources.